W9-CCS-689

Table of Contents

Leadership in Sports

Visioning for Organizations/Events

Sports Tourism Marketing

Events and Event Bids

Dedications

To those that came before me.
Thank you for showing me the way.

To those that walk with me.
Thank you for your energy and continued support along the journey.

To those that will come after me.
Thank you for picking up the torch.

To my wife Sharon.
Thank you for always believing in me.
Even when I didn't believe in myself.

"Champions are made from something they have deep inside them…..a desire, a dream, a vision."
-- Muhammad Ali

"Become a Leadership CHAMPion"

There are thousands of commentaries about the core traits that define a great leader. Theories abound on what makes one person a leader, and another a follower. As sports industry professionals we are all accountable as leaders in one way or another. We lead event Local Organizing Committees (LOCs), special projects, direct reports, volunteer teams, and our organizations as a whole. As a leader, we must always be sharpening our skills in preparation for the next big challenge.

In our work with our various clients, we are often asked to evaluate the organization's environment, both internally and externally. This process often uncovers the rock star team members, the ones who are truly leading the effort day in and day out – the Champions of the organization. These talented individuals come in many shapes and sizes, however most we find embody five key characteristics that make them a leadership CHAMPion……

Collaborator – George W. Bush once said, "A leader is someone who brings people together." The ability to work with others and build working teams is a vital tool for all great leaders. At the Huddle Up Group, we believe this is the single most important trait of successful people (and companies). You can't always do it on your own; you need others to participate to reach your long-term goals. The ability to collaborate is critical to that end.

Humility – One of the most difficult things to do is to stand back and give credit to others. After all, we work in sports, where competition is part of the job. We all want to "win" and personal acclimation comes with success. The best leaders are those that not only can easily attribute victory to the team as a whole, but they can also take the blame when things go poorly (even if it wasn't their fault). By their nature, humble people are well equipped to garner buy-in and lead organizations to prosperity. They make it about the team and not the individual, creating an atmosphere rich in partnership and teamwork – which in the end leads to high achievement.

Action-oriented – The top people in any field are not afraid to take action. Of course some leaders take longer to map out their game plans, but once the goals are identified, leaders aggressively launch into action. For leaders, mistakes are simply part of the process, so there is no fear of activating an initiative.

Mentorship – Leaders think about the long-term, not just tomorrow. In order to have sustainable success leaders must not only continually improve their own performance, but also grow the skills of those around them. Mentorship, for both the leader and the follower, is critical to continually raise the bar. We find that the cream of the crop in our industry make time not only to mentor their followers, but also to be mentored by others.

Preparation – Alexander Graham Bell, Abraham Lincoln, Colin Powell, Arthur Ashe…..These men all cite preparation as the most important key to success. Great leaders not only prepare, but they often over-prepare. That is they go to extreme measures to know everything about a situation. For instance in a bid process, your preparation may include: determining the decision makers (a person or a committee?), what are their major event priorities (venue condition or volunteer management?), what is the financial agreement for the championship (bid fee or venue rental assistance, shared P/L?), what can we add that will make the event the best of its kind (athlete and official hospitality?). There is a saying lawyers use when talking about trying a case in court: "Don't ever ask a question that you don't already know the answer to." To a certain extent, this is also true in the sports tourism and events industry. We should never go into a meeting or a planning process without having all the information we need to achieve success. For great leaders, preparation is every bit as important as execution.

Collaborate, be humble, take action, mentor and be mentored, and prepare for success. No matter your position in the sports tourism and events industry, these are the elements that will lead to sustained success. These five characteristics combine to make leaders into CHAMPions.

Discussion Questions

1. What leadership traits to think are most important? Why?
2. If you ranked your personal skill set on each of the Leadership CHAMPion characteristics, which ones do you consider strengths? Which ones do you consider weaknesses?
3. Who are the best leaders you have ever worked with? Why were they great leaders?

Supplemental Reading

Inc. writer Kevin Daum offers his top ten list of great leadership traits: http://www.inc.com/kevin-daum/10-traits-of-great-leaders-and-their-followers.html.

II

"Seek the blame, give away the fame."
-- Miles Anthony Smith

"Leadership Sucks"

On one of our weekly date nights, my wife offered up a rather poignant statement. After a particularly rough day at the office, she said "Sometimes being a leader really sucks." For those in leadership positions, this surely isn't a new concept. If you are a sports executive, an event director, a non-profit manager, a parent, a teacher, or the CEO of a Fortune 500 company, yes, leadership has its challenges.

If we turn things around, what are the great benefits of being a leader? Also, what leadership traits make the team or company better than its peers? We offer you five concepts that make leadership worth it all.....

1. **Servitude** – The best leaders put their mission and their team first. Individual acclaim for these leaders comes later, if at all. Their focus is always on the group's goal and not their own gain. This is one of the most fulfilling parts of leading. When you do something alone, there are very few people to share it with. When you achieve something collectively, you have a group of contributors to celebrate with side by side.
2. **Support** – Great leaders will drop everything to help their followers. In turn their teams will feel more enabled and supported, which will lead them to be more successful over time. When people feel safe and that someone has their back, they become amazingly effective.
3. **Collaboration** – Leadership comes with strings. You need to deal with every task that comes your way, whether you have the resources or not. Great leaders find a way to partner with others in

order to attract the support they need. Collaboration leads to winning teams.

4. **Delegation** – Have you ever delegated a key project or task to someone on your team and watched them flourish? It's one of the great feelings of working with others, watching someone else accomplish something great. If you haven't experienced it, try it. Great delegation can not only change your attitude about leadership, but you can learn a great deal about the human condition.

5. **Promote Others** – Team success is about the greater good. Individual accomplishment can still be part of the larger picture, but not if one person trumps the others. When possible, promote the work of your followers and the collective team. Propping up those that do the work behind the scenes not only builds them up, but strengthens the overall foundation of your organization.

These tactics are easy to implement in any organization. However it takes the commitment of those at the top. Make time to check your work. Put these strategies in your daily schedule and make sure you review them consistently as a check point. Small advances in these areas will yield huge gains over time.

Yes, sometimes leadership is challenging, but more often than not, the leadership cloud has a silver lining. Serve your stakeholders, support your team, collaborate with your constituents, delegate to others, and promote your followers. Exercise these five keys to success, and leadership won't suck.

Discussion Questions

1. What projects currently on your plate can you delegate?
2. How do you recognize the work of others on your team?
3. What are your keys to collaborating with others?

Supplemental Reading

Business leaders and columnist Harvey Mackay offers his six keys to great delegation:
http://www.inc.com/harvey-mackay/6-keys-effective-delegation.html.

III

"Difficulties are meant to rouse, not discourage. The human spirit is to grow strong by conflict."
-- William Ellery Channing

"The Virtual Bench"

Late summer in our home state of Arizona brings with it monsoon season. Every afternoon the clouds roll in and Mother Nature takes over. While these storms are quite turbulent, they are normally harmless beyond a few lightning bolts and a strong downpour of rain in a short window of time. However, one storm created an issue for our family. When the storm hit we were at our church, just down the street from our house. When we walk to church each week we use the electric garage door to get in and out of our house. The storm knocked out power in the neighborhood, and made our garage door inoperable. We didn't have any keys with us, so we couldn't get back into the house after church. The power was out for more than 90 minutes, so we were completely isolated from the world for that time (no cell phones, no computers, no TV, I didn't have my wallet or access to the car). The moral of the story.....have a back-up plan.

In the business world we need to have alternative plans when things don't work out the way we had predicted. Nowhere is this more important than in building our work teams. As we accumulate talented team members, over time they will have additional opportunities. This is especially true of non-profit organizations like DMOs that often hire young (affordable) talent. Eventually they will build their skills and be recruited by others to move to a new position elsewhere. In these cases, we need a back-up plan. We need a virtual bench.

The concept of the virtual bench is to continuously recruit talent. You may not have a staff vacancy today, but at some point you will, so we need to constantly be on the lookout for the next key acquisition. The virtual bench represents the people that you would go to if a staffing (or board) need arises. Ask yourself, if your top sales person left tomorrow morning, who would you call? What about your lead event services manager? What if your board chair had to step down mid-term? If they left, do you know who you would recruit to fill the hole? We recommend that you ask this question of everyone on your team; both board and staff.....Even about yourself. If you left, what is the game plan? If there isn't one, and you want your legacy to survive your departure, help build the succession plan for the organization.

In order to build a sustainable organization, we need to continually fill the pipeline with talent. Talented staff, talented volunteers, talented partners, talented everything. We always need to build our virtual benches and be ready to leap into action when there is a need. Think of it as if you are an athletic director and your head football coach just left for another school. Do you have a list of candidates in the top desk drawer ready to go? As leaders we should always be ready for change. Signer Gwen Stefani once said, "Let's be realistic, it's not going to be like this forever." Take time to cultivate your virtual bench. The more time and resources you spend on this process now, the better position you will be in when change comes in the future.

Discussion Questions

1. Do you have a succession plan for everyone in your organization?
2. How do you cultivate relationships to populate your virtual bench?
3. If you left your organization, what would happen?

Supplemental Reading

Author Joel McCabe offers his strategies to creating a virtual bench: http://www.salesbenchmarkindex.com/bid/104781/Key-to-Hire-A-Players-Use-a-Virtual-Bench.

IV

"It's how you handle adversity, not how it affects you."
-- President Bill Clinton

"Handling Adversity"

On a business trip I 2014, a late night flight I was on was cancelled due to weather. We were loaded up on the plane ready to go, and were then asked to de-plane and return to the terminal. It was the last connecting flight to my final destination that day. It was nearly midnight, and the next flight out was at 8 AM the following day. With such an early flight out the next morning, at best I would be able to get a quick nap at an area hotel (or stay in the terminal and sleep there). I opted for the former and booked a room at a nearby Holiday Inn. On the shuttle ride to the hotel I was calm and at peace. There was little stress about the inconvenience, and I was already planning out the timeline for the following day.

We had a full day of meetings scheduled should the weather clear and allow our morning flight to land. Luckily, after two more delays, we were cleared to fly to my final destination. The plane landed thirty minutes before meeting number one (plenty of time). I was a bit tired come dinner time, otherwise the day came off without a hitch. Luckily the plane schedule worked out and the weather finally cooperated. Mission accomplished.

Later that day I called home to check in. My wife Sharon, a seasoned traveler herself, told me that five years ago I wouldn't have handled this series of events nearly as well. I have to say, I agree with her. Of course with age comes patience, but missing planes and having your travels interrupted can be quite frustrating. So what lessons can we take from this experience? Here are the three things I think have helped me deal with adversity more effectively today than in years past:

1. Only fret over things you can control – There are things you can impact and things you cannot. In the case of the bad weather on my recent trip, the pilot's job is to get us to our destination safely. The pilots (or ticket counter staff) can't control the weather, neither can you. There is no need to spend your emotional capital battling something that is out of your hands.
2. Be calm and polite when adversity strikes – In the case of a cancelled flight (or similar occurrence) you will need someone else's help to re-book you and to put your travels back on the right track. We will get further with honey than with vinegar in this instance. Rather than dump your issues on someone else, take a deep breath, explain the situation, and thank them in advance for whatever help they can offer.
3. Help those around you when they go on "tilt" – I've found it very soothing to talk to people in adverse conditions and let them get their pains out in the open. Usually these are the people that are yelling at gate agents about the weather or a late plane (last I checked airline employees can't alter the atmosphere). In talking to these people, we not only allow them to target someone else, but we free the airline employees in this case to do their job and get everyone re-booked. This often has a calming effect on the person causing the commotion. Take one for the team here and let them direct their scorn at you rather than someone else.

We are all works in progress. So are those around us. When we face tough circumstances, remember that there are others in the same boat. Stay positive, manage what we can control to the best of our abilities, and remember we are not the only person on earth facing adversity that day. Keep in mind, no matter how bad you think you have it, there is always someone who would trade places with you.

Discussion Questions

1. What tactics do you employ to positively deal with adverse conditions?
2. Talk about an adverse situation that you have faced in the past. What helped you resolve the problem?
3. Who is the best person you know at disarming disputes? What do they do that allows them to be great in this area?

Supplemental Reading

Here is an article by Harry Shade about coping with adversity: http://innovisionglobal.com/index.php/resources/articles/the-three-simple-steps-to-dealing-with-adversity.html.

V

"The single biggest problem in communication is the illusion that it has taken place."
-- George Bernard Shaw

"Teamwork through Communication"

During the 2014 NFL season, Peyton Manning led the Denver Broncos to the Superbowl in New York. In the weeks leading up to the big game, much was been made about Manning's signal call of "Omaha! Omaha!" Manning's high level of communication is legendary. This advanced level of communication is not only necessary to run a complicated NFL offense, but is every bit as important to sports industry professionals in leading our organizations.

As an avid football fan (and the son of a football coach), I'm still no expert on the nuances of running an offense. However, I think we can all gain insights from watching an elite quarterback run his business and apply those to our daily lives. Here are four communication skills that we can steal from Peyton Manning:

1. **Be clear** – At the line of scrimmage, Manning's voice is discernable and forceful. He balances the play calls with hand signals to make sure everyone is on the same page before the snap. Even after he has called a play, he is still talking to his teammates to make sure they know where to be and what is coming next. His message is easily understood, which limits mistakes by teammates.
2. **Be concise** – Great leaders are very specific about the results they are looking to achieve. Those that make their goals transparent

and communicate those effectively to their followers are more apt to achieve success.

3. **Be direct** – There is little wasted time or energy in calling a play and getting the ball snapped. You only have 40 seconds on the play clock, so there is little time to waste. In our communications with our work teams, cut through the clutter and get right to the point. Time is a valuable asset. Cut to the chase and make the most of it.

4. **Be prompt** – Communication needs to be delivered in a timely fashion for someone to utilize the information. If someone is waiting on information to keep a project moving ahead, the chances of success diminish with each passing moment. A great goal is to try to never have anyone waiting on you. Get out in front of projects and stay there.

Even though the Broncos Superbowl run fell short that year, much can be learned from the combatants. The coaches and the quarterbacks are technically the CEOs of their teams. The team that communicates their game plan in the most effective manner usually wins the Lombardi Trophy. We all have our personal goals, our own Superbowls to win. Learn from the best, in sports and in life, put their examples to work, and hoist that trophy.

Discussion Questions

1. Who is the best communicator you have ever encountered? What about them makes them a great communicator?
2. How do you communicate best to your stakeholders?
3. What can you do to be a better communicator?

VI

"The way positive reinforcement is carried out is more important than the amount."
-- B. F. Skinner

"The Powers of Three"

Leadership is the most studied subject matter in industry. There have been thousands upon thousands of studies conducted on the traits that "all" great leaders possess. Of course, not every leader is cut from the same cloth, which is what most of the academic research inevitably concludes. Even within disciplines (like rights holders, sports commissions, convention bureaus, or national governing bodies) there are numerous styles of leadership that have proven successful.

If you have worked with Huddle Up Group in the past, you will know that we build our recommendations and activation plans around what we call the "Powers of Three." We present our clients with three major initiatives, with no more than three action items for each initiative. We believe that in nearly all cases, focusing on more than three deeply rooted strategies will lead to diluted efforts (and results) in too many areas. Most often, by taking action in the three areas that need the most attention, all of the small issues disappear over time. Limit the areas of emphasis, stay focused, and increase positive results.

Applying the Powers of Three concept to the vast subject of leadership could lead to a very diverse list of responses. We offer our view here. Our opinion on the three most important traits for great leadership in the sports tourism and events industry include:

1. Collaboration – We believe that teamwork and the ability to work with others is THE single most important trait to successful leadership. If you are reading this publication, you likely work in sports tourism and events. Our industry is a team activity. There is no place on earth where collaboration is more important than in sports, whether in a team game or in hosting a national championship.

2. Passion – If you don't have a passion for what you are doing, try something else. Leading anything with a lack of enthusiasm is difficult, even for the most accomplished professionals. Most people punch the clock every day to go to jobs that they look upon as a way to make a living. We have the opportunity every day to work in and around sport. The mere fact that we get paid to do things others would volunteer to do is proof that we are truly blessed to work in this industry. Bring passion to your work and make the most of every opportunity to lead.

3. Positivity – Okay, so "positivity" isn't a real word, but we all know it when we see it. Having a positive attitude towards a person's surroundings, especially when things look dire, serves as a great example to those around us. Who do you want to lead your organization/event/team when the chips are down? When things get tough, do you want the person who sulks or becomes a negative influence, or do you want the person who smiles and says, "We can do this, let's go"? It's a rhetorical question, but I'd suggest you choose the latter option.

Former General Electric CEO Jack Welch once said, "Before you are a leader, success is all about growing yourself. When you become a leader, success is all about growing others." No matter where are in life's leadership continuum, you are either being impacted by others or mentoring someone yourself. And it's likely that you are doing both simultaneously. While Welch offers great perspective, we believe we are all leaders and followers -- at the same time.

It's easy to fall into the trap of thinking "I'm not the director (or CEO) so I don't lead anyone." We all lead someone, even if that is only oneself. So whether you subscribe to our proposed Powers of Three, or to Jack Welch, or to one of the thousands of other leadership models, one thing is certain: we have the ability to lead those around us in a very positive way. Sometimes you may realize that you are leading others, sometimes you might not. But we must all be cognizant that our actions speak on our behalf. Working well with others, showing great passion, and exhibiting superior enthusiasm are but three ways to lead. You have your own style, your own Powers of Three. Identify them, enhance them, unleash them, lead with them.

Discussion Questions

1. Talk about your most successful collaborations. What contributed to the success of that project?
2. Name three ways you can show positive reinforcement to a team member.
3. What are the "Powers of Three" for your organization? Does everyone on the team know those to be the three important focus areas of the company?

VII

"Invisible threads are the strongest ties."
-- Friedrich Nietzsche

"Sports Business Manifesto"

Most leaders have some form of guiding principle list through which they run their organizations. These "manifestos" often provide structure for partnerships, operations, and overall management of the company in question.

Recently, a friend of the Huddle Up Group sent us his top ten rules for sports business management. Since we all love lists, below is Ross Balling's manifesto (Ross is the President of Sales and Marketing for the Extreme Volleyball Professionals Tour)......

1. Put everything on the table.
2. Partners are good for reducing expenses thus increasing net profit and stability for your event or company.
3. Referrals and renewals are what we work so hard for.
4. If an agreement is for less than $10,000 in revenue, but has more than one page of deliverables, don't sign it.
5. If a good client says the check is in the mail, then the check is in the mail.
6. Sports Commissions are solid partners for event operators.
7. Dates are important.
8. If you have the right partner, money is never the road block.
9. Athletes play in all weather. Fans do not.
10.   Exclusivity is wrong; right to work means business.

Ross' list is outstanding and offers several straight forward insights into partnership development and management. We would add five more to his list.....

1. If things don't add up now, they won't later.
2. Those that didn't deliver last time, won't deliver next time.
3. Work with people you trust.
4. Talk openly about your goals.
5. Trust your gut.

Guiding principles are critical for long-term success. They help guide decisions and actions to create consistency within an organization. Write them down, advertise them, talk about them, do everything you can to make them tangible to everyone that comes into contact with you and your company.

Discussion Questions

1. What items would be on your sports business manifesto?
2. Review the above manifesto. Anything you disagree with? Why?
3. Talk about the best partnership you have today. What is great about it?

Supplemental Reading

Branding expert Téa Silvestre offers up this article on how to build your own business manifesto - http://thewordchef.com/2012/08/manifesto-why-how-write-yours/.

VIII

"Vision is the art of seeing what is invisible to others."
-- Jonathan Swift

"Three Circles of Vision"

One of the most important decisions organizations face each day is what NOT to do. Sometimes opportunities present themselves that we should say no to. New business ideas, potential partnerships, or chances for expanding your company, often times the best decisions are those that we don't make.

Blogger Bud Caddell recently penned a three circle diagram that looks at how we should evaluate opportunities and our organizations.

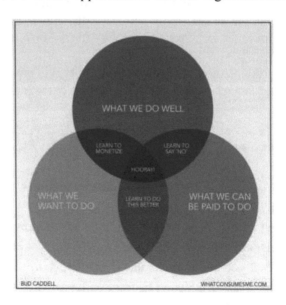

The "Venn Diagram" as it is known (pictured) is a series of intersections between three key thoughts:

1. What we do well.
2. What we want to do.
3. What we can get paid to do.

The ultimate situation is where we can intersect all three areas and achieve great success. However, in our opinion, the more important component of the Venn Diagram is learning to say "no".

Think back on your experiences. Remember a big decision you had to make where you almost made a big mistake? In hindsight, what would have happened if you had made that choice? How would your business have been affected?

While Caddell's diagram is somewhat simplistic, we can all use it as a compass in making big decisions. Is the new opportunity a fit with what we do well? Will we be able to monetize it effectively? Is it something we actually want to do and have the capacity to take on?

If not, just say "no". Another (better) opportunity will come along in the future for those who are patient and stick to their game plan on the big decisions.

Discussion Questions

1. What big decision did you NOT make that in hindsight was the right call?
2. Talk about a time where you should have taken more time to make a big decision. What was the outcome? What would you do differently if you had to make that decision again?
3. If you built your own Venn Diagram on leadership, what elements would make up your three circles?

IX

"The first principle of contract negotiations is don't remind them of what you did in the past - tell them what you're going to do in the future."
-- Stan Musial

"The Art of Negotiation"

Business leadership expert Marty Latz once wrote an article outlining the best practices of negotiation. The article was centered on former NBA player-coach-announcer Doug Collins, and offered some great insights. Collins outlined several tips to negotiation that I believe we can all apply to the sports events industry. Here are three of the tips that Collins offered:

1. Keep the end goal in mind – Both sides have a desired end result. Each side has a "home run" outcome they want to achieve. Collins advises us to not focus on what other deals look like, but focus on the win-win outcome for the particular deal you are working on.
2. Negotiate through truth and trust – This is all about transparency. The more up front and transparent you are about your position and your goals, the easier it is for the person across the table to trust you and for you to move towards a common ground.
3. Relationships impact the negotiation process – As we have discussed in past columns, taking time to build strong relationships can help in all areas of our profession. There is likely no area where this rings true more than in the negotiation process. If you have a foundation to build on through a strong personal or business relationship, you will be able to negotiate in good faith to reach a wining result.

Negotiation is a big part of our everyday lives. It's part of our jobs, our friendships, and our family life. In order to have consistent success we must become expert negotiators. Doug Collin's thoughts on the end goal, truth and trust, and strong relationships are paramount to finding win-win scenarios in life. I would even add one more – positive thought.

To truly negotiate we must believe in our hearts that a great outcome will be the end result. We must enter into any negotiation with a positive attitude and a mentality that any barrier can (and will) be overcome. Transparency, trustful relationships, and positive thought. Put those elements in play and championship-level success will be reached.

Discussion Questions

1. What do you believe are the most important elements of negotiation?
2. Talk about negotiations you have participated in that ended well. What do you believe contributed to that outcome?
3. Talk about negotiations you have participated in that ended poorly. What do you believe contributed to that outcome?

X

"Difficulties are the spice that gives success its full flavor."
-- Unknown

"Three Steps to Success"

Every Sunday my wife and I read the paper in the kitchen. It is a highlight to our week. We both happen to be born under the sign of Pisces so one of the common areas of the paper we both read is the weekly horoscope. One horoscope entry from 2014 was applicable not only to everyday lives, but also to those that work in sports tourism and events. Paraphrasing the entry, it read, "Keep it simple. Success involves only three steps, (1) say what you are going to do, (2) do it, and (3) repeat."

I'm sure as you read this you say "well sure, everyone knows that." As I read and re-read the simplicity of this game plan, I realized this is exactly what we try and focus our clients on every day at the Huddle Up Group: focus and simplicity. But what really jumps out at me in this three step format is this......We see many communities and rights holders that don't know how to address step number one, "say what you are going to do." If you cannot define and easily communicate step one, the following steps are meaningless.

It seems so simple, but how often do we sit down as an organization and say "what are we all about, what are our goals, and can we define them so everyone can understand them?" In many cases, the answer to these questions varies based on who you ask. This means as leaders we all fail.

As we approach this important visioning task for our organizations, we offer a challenge to each of us.....answer the simple question in step number one.... "What are we going to do?" The answer to this question is not a mission statement, but should be able to address three things:

1. What is it that your organization offers to our industry that nobody else can?
2. What goals do we have that our constituents can understand?
3. What tactics or methods do we use to achieve the goals?

It's a simple outline, however the devil is in the details. Does your organization have a definitive statement that addresses step number one and also answers the three "what" questions listed above? Does your board know how to communicate what it is your organization does every day and why? Do your sponsors know what they are investing in and why? Does your staff know why you make the decisions you make and what the end goal is each day? For destination management organizations (DMOs), sports commissions, or rights holders to be successful, our entire network of stakeholders should be able to easily communicate a statement that answers the steps and also the "what" questions. Suddenly this isn't as easy a task.

As leaders it is our responsibility to own the direction of our organizations, our events, our boards, our staffs, and our constituents. We need to undertake this exercise on a regular basis, if nothing else than to recalibrate where we stand and to make sure our stakeholders are on board with our vision. If we don't take this constant re-evaluation seriously, we may find ourselves in the "we have always done it this way" position. This is a recipe to grow tired and to allow other more progressive organizations to take control of our market share.

Discussion Questions

1. Write out your organization's answers to step one ("What are we going to do?").
2. What is it that your organization offers to our industry that nobody else can?
3. How do you message your mission to stakeholders?

XI

"You have to learn the rules of the game, and then you have to play better than anyone else."
-- Albert Einstein

"Game Changer"

One of the great fictional characters of all time, Captain James Tiberius Kirk of the Starship Enterprise, hated losing so much he actually changed the rules of the game. For Star Trek fans, you will remember the tale of the "Kobayashi Maru, No Win Scenario." In the television show and later in the movie series, the Kobayashi Maru was a training exercise in a flight simulator for future leaders of star fleet command. The exercise is programmed by a computer to offer the captain (in this case Kirk) zero possible outcomes of success. Basically, the ship crashes and the crew dies no matter what the captain does, thusly a "no win scenario" (the Maru was so popular with Star Trek fans it even has its own Wikipedia page).

Our fearless Captain Kirk, having failed the test on numerous occasions, became the first and only person to ever defeat the Kobayashi Maru. On the eve of the exam, Kirk changed the program to offer a winning outcome. While he was reprimanded for essentially cheating on the test, he was also commended for creative thinking. Kirk changed the game.

As sports industry professionals, we rarely encounter "no win scenarios", but we can still learn from William Shatner's character. We must always look for winning opportunities to change the playing field and slant the outcome in the favor of our destinations. Here is one real life example I have seen that achieved a game changing outcome.

In 1999, the Western Athletic Conference (WAC) had 16 teams and was the country's first collegiate super conference. That year a core group of members from the WAC left to start their own league, known as the

Mountain West Conference. The departure of these members presented some challenges for the WAC, and an opportunity for our sports commission in Tulsa.

The University of Nevada Las Vegas (UNLV) was part of the group that left for the new conference. UNLV at the time was the long running host of the WAC basketball championship. With their departure, essentially the history of the event, its sponsor support, and the arena it was played in, moved to the new Mountain West Conference along with UNLV. The WAC had to find a new home for their marquee event, and replace the financial loss of its title sponsor.

The WAC issued an RFP to all of their members, including the University of Tulsa. The RFP was for two years. Seven schools, some with their DMOs and sports commissions, put forth bids. Our bid in Tulsa, with the University and the Sports Commission as partners, was very unique in three ways. One, we brought a title sponsor to the table as part of our bid. If the tournament was played in Tulsa, the title sponsor would commit cash and other resources to support the event. We changed the game.

Second, our title sponsor put terms in the agreement that the tournament would need to be in Tulsa for three years rather than the two that were in the RFP. That too changed the game.

Lastly, in putting together our presentation, one member of our team asked what turned out to be a very important question, "What is the order of presentations for the seven cities, and how long does each have?" The answer was we (Tulsa) were last of the seven cities to present and each city got an hour. That meant the athletic directors and administrators would be in a hotel conference room ALL DAY covering the same information over and over. We anticipated that by the time we got in there, they would be zombies. We had to change the game for them to take notice of our bid.

When we entered the presentation area, in lieu of suits we were wearing tuxedos and tennis shoes, and the four of us that presented came in whooping and hollering and throwing Nerf basketballs all over the room. We got their attention, we had fun with it, and we charged up the audience. We opened our presentation by saying (essentially), "We appreciate the time you have spent in this room all day, and we want to respect that." We used less than half our time, hit the key points, and then had one of our community leaders ask for the sale. He did so by saying, "I'm a volunteer, here to invite you to our city. We are up here in these costumes which I get is odd, but we wanted to really grab your attention, knowing you have been here all day. Costumes or not, one thing I can tell you about the people in Tulsa is that they are VERY good at what they do and this will be the biggest event in our city when you are there. Thank you for your time, we'd love to have you in Tulsa. I hope you can use the time we left for a well-deserved break" and we walked out.

The WAC awarded us the tournament for three years when the RFP only had two up for bid. At that time it was a big deal for our destination. We changed the game, and the WAC leadership responded positively. There are opportunities for people in our industry to change the game every day. Where the opportunity presents itself, let's be like Captain Kirk and create winning scenarios even when one doesn't appear to exist.

Discussion Questions

1. What challenges do you face in your current role?
2. How can you change the game to address these challenges?
3. Discuss a time where you came up with a creative way to handle a tough situation.

XII

"People may cancel a family vacation, but they are not going to cancel their trip for little Susie who qualified for a championship."
-- Mathew Payne

The Importance of Sports Tourism

According to Sports Events Magazine's 2014 Market Report, the grass roots sports tourism industry is a $8.9 billion economic engine. The growth of this market segment over the past twenty years has been driven by several key factors:

1. As many in the industry have pointed out over the years, youth sporting events are relatively immune to market trends that impact other areas of tourism. Things like a bad economy, war, high unemployment, and 9/11 rarely find their way into the youth sports marketplace. Grass roots sports tourism is a unifier in our country, and few parents will deprive their children from participating in regional and national tournaments if their kids are given the opportunity to compete.

2. As companies cut back on annual meetings and corporate travel, the number of youth sporting events (and the number of athletes participating in those events) has increased year over year for nearly two decades. Statistics Canada says the amateur sporting events space is the fastest growing segment of the Canadian tourism industry. This sentiment holds true for many regions around the United States as well, with the mid and smaller markets experiencing the most growth (Sports Tourism Magazine). Thusly, the competition from cities, sports commissions, and DMOs to get a piece of this market has reached an all-time high.

3. Sports are a tremendous economic development tool. The level of investment needed to conduct a U14 soccer tournament is relatively low when compared to infrastructure that must be built to relocate a company to your community (or to host a mega event like a Super Bowl, Olympics, etc.). A sustained effort in this grass roots space can lead to annual returns that make a big difference in the host communities of these events. With little investment (opportunity cost) the host regions for these events drive significant economic impact to the area, leverage the investment that has been made in existing facilities, employ local citizens, and drive sales to the community's businesses.

4. The benefits of hosting grass roots events year over year don't stop at the importing of new tourist dollars into the local economy. In hosting major national events, the host community often receives wide spread recognition through various media outlets (new media and traditional channels). This marketing reach is often something the community couldn't buy if it had an "unlimited" advertising budget. The recognition in hosting these events often leads to return visits of the participants and their families, new visits by those exposed to the increased media reach, and increased interest from rights holders to host future events at the destination.

Researcher Heather Gibson of the University of Florida once cited the need for "better coordination among agencies responsible for sport and those responsible for tourism" and she called for a cease fire on "territorial contests between departments claiming tourism expertise and those claiming sport expertise." Today, sports tourism is big business, and no more so should we heed Ms. Gibson's recommendations than in the mid and small markets where grass roots sporting events make the largest impact. A unified community strategy can yield championship level results for our destinations. If we want our destinations to attract our share of the sports tourism pie, we need to work together in developing a strategy for sustainable success.

Discussion Qutesions

1. Talk about terriroty issues you face within your organziation.
2. Discuss territory issues you face externally.
3. What strategies have you used to unify your community/industry?

XIII

"The customer's perception is your reality."
-- Kate Zabriskie

Fantastic Customer Service – The Beer Guy

Over the years we have touched upon several cases of organizations with, shall we say, challenging service and marketing activities. This writing is the exact opposite. This is the story of "Mark the Beer Guy."

Each year, tens of thousands of fans flock to Arizona in March for the Cactus League – Major League Baseball's Spring Training. The Cactus League accounts for more than $300 million annually to the State of Arizona. It's a great opportunity to show off the State, and also a platform to offer our customers fantastic customer service.

Nearing the end of the Spring Training one season, we made a trip to an Oakland A's game with some our sports community leaders. It was there we met Mark The Beer Guy (check him out on Twitter @MarkBeerGuy). Mark immediately struck up a conversation, then handed us his baseball card. Let that sit in for a minute. The beer guy has his own baseball card, "limited edition" none the less. The card was of course autographed. The card included his vital statistics (6-foot 7-inches, 283 pounds, pours right, throws peanuts right), his contact information, a QR code, as well as a list of events he has worked in the past (three Superbowls, a World Series, the Stanley Cup Finals, an MLB All-Star Game – he sold hot dogs – and the first event he ever worked – the 1980 Minnesota Twins home opener). This guy is a professional suds slinger.

Awe struck at the concept of a beer guy with a baseball card, we somehow ordered a round of cold ones. As Mark departed, he said "when you want another one tweet me and I'll be here in no time" (his twitter handle was on the baseball card he left with us). Guess how many vendors we dealt with that day. You guessed it, one. Mark the Beer Guy. He got all our business and all of our tips that day.

As leaders of our organizations, there is an opportunity for us to market ourselves creatively and to offer fantastic customer service. What is on your baseball card?

Discussion Questions

1. Brainstorm three unique marketing ideas to promote your organization.
2. Build a budget for the top idea.
3. What channels of delivery do you need to launch the promotion? Launch it.

Supplemental Reading

Here is a link to Mark's baseball card "collection" - http://www.markthebeerguy.com/cards.html.

"PRACTICE as if you are the WORST, PERFORM as if you are the BEST."
-- Jaspher Kantuna

"Worst Practices of Sports Tourism"

We were once invited to present at a regional tourism conference. The conference's theme was of course, sports tourism. Over 250 C-level tourism leaders attended the event, most of which were trying to capitalize on the growing market that is grass roots sports tourism.

In our work consulting many destination marketing organizations and sports commissions, we delve into the ways that our clients market themselves. We also talk to event rights holders and national governing bodies to ask them how they view certain communities, and what they look for in a host city. From these fact finding efforts, we have drawn several themes on what NOT to do when promoting a destination in the sports tourism marketplace.

We offer you five "Worst Practices" in selling your destination to event rights holders:

1. Creating a "Brand" without a plan – If you have ever watched the television show Shark Tank, you know what we mean here. Brands are not built with a pretty logo and a new business card. They are built with results, which in our case, means sales. Landing and properly executing events in your destination will build your brand, not some creative guy in an expensive agency downtown.
2. Adding "Sports Sales" to someone's title – Taking a SMURF person and adding "Sports" to their title does not put your destination in the sports tourism game. Event rights holders will

see right through that. Resist the temptation to put "sales" in anyone's title and make sure the people that you send to sports trade shows know sports. If they don't, your potential clients will know that your intention is a heads in beds play and will likely move on to another community that understands their event needs.

3. Employing the "Funnel" approach – You must avoid the often used method of filling your sales funnel hoping that some business will eventually fall out of the bottom. The thought that more leads mean more room nights is not true in sports. In sports, better RELATIONSHIPS lead to more events which lead to more room nights.

4. Disregarding community – Sports can bring more people to the table than the general hospitality industry might. Your community has folks in it that wouldn't likely support tourism, but will support SPORTS. Use sports to tap into these new resources.

5. Putting room nights ahead of the event – If room nights are your priority, rights holders can smell it a mile away. Sports also have a greater opportunity to revisit certain host cities than one-off conventions do. Put on a great event and they will come back soon, most often in a year or two. Many conventions come to a community once then don't return for decades. It's easier to get more business from a happy client than it is to find a new one. Room nights will be realized, but the event has to come first. Put on a good event and the fruits of that effort will be borne over the long haul.

We often talk about authenticity in marketing. No place is this more important than the sales process. Use knowledgeable people to sell your brand, bring in new resources by placing sport ahead of room nights, and build long-term relationships by putting the event first. If you do these things, you will see great sports tourism results in your destination.

Discussion Questions

1. What tactics does your organization employ to build relationships with the decision makers of sport?
2. Who leads your sports sales efforts? What is their title? What sport knowledge/expertise do they possess?
3. Who is the best sports tourism organization that you see in the marketplace? What do they do that your organization does not?

Supplemental Reading

Customer service expert Micah Solomon offers his ten worst practices for customer service (we like the bonus tip for item number ten, "Not realizing the beginning starts before the beginning") - http://www.forbes.com/sites/micahsolomon/2014/07/14/the-10-all-time-worst-customer-service-practices/.

"It's how you handle adversity, not how it affects you."
-- William J. Clinton

"Alligators and Authenticity"

In 2015, the Greater Phoenix area hosted the Pro Bowl, the PGA Tour's Phoenix Open, and the Superbowl – all over the span of eight days. It was a great week for our home community, both economically and in terms of worldwide exposure (the Huddle Up Group is based in Phoenix). As the week began, there was some controversy, and we are not talking about the Patriots and deflate-gate.

One of the Superbowl's largest sponsors made a rather large gaffe. Pepsi had developed commercials for the game and also plastered billboards all around town depicting parts of Arizona that are more than 300 miles from the host site. No, not the Grand Canyon, which of course is an iconic Arizona landmark. The backdrop photos used are simply rock formations that are in remote areas of our state (some members of the media suggested they might even be photos of Utah). Pepsi missed the mark, and social media let them know (http://www.azcentral.com/story/entertainment/events/super-bowl/2015/01/23/social-media-critics-say-halftime-ads-feature-wrong-valley/22253891/).

Right around this time, I had the opportunity to try something new: alligator. A restaurant in our area serves several unique entrees, one of which is the ferocious reptile. The waitress told us people say that alligator is "like chicken but more chewy" which wasn't really a testament to how good (and different) the dish proved to be. That said, Alligator deserves an authentic summary of its great taste and its dis-similarity from poultry. The key word is "authentic."

Years ago in Denver, the NBA hosted its annual All-Star weekend in the Mile High City. In the discussions leading up to the event, the one thing that the community told the league over and over was to present Denver as the hip, young, tech driven town that it is. Community leaders did not want to be portrayed as a western cow town. Who did the NBA hire as the halftime entertainment? LeAnn Rimes and Big and Rich (see "Cowtown"). NOT authentic to who Denver was then and is today. Big miss by the NBA.

Alligators and the NBA aside, we should always strive towards authenticity. Personally, professionally, how we work with clients, and the overall way we conduct ourselves. The Superbowl Pepsi ads were not authentic to Greater Phoenix. For a community to put so much into hosting America's biggest event, the sponsors of the NFL needed to be more accountable for their messaging. For a company as large (and as smart) as Pepsi to act in such an autonomous way is irresponsible to the community that is opening its arms to them in hosting the big game. They should have been more engaging in the creative process and made sure their representation of our community passed the authenticity sniff test.

Discussion Questions

1. How do you market your organization/community authentically?
2. If you were Pepsi and the media picked up on the ill-fated billboard photos, what would you have done to solve the problem?
3. What social media protocols do you have in place to be consistently present to manage your brand?

Supplemental Reading

Professor Herminia Ibarra has done research on the topic of authenticity in leadership. One of her best articles on the topic ran in the Harvard Business Review - https://hbr.org/2015/01/the-authenticity-paradox.

XVI

"Marketing is too important to be left to the marketing department."
-- David Packard

Ducks On The Pond

Over the past two decades the membership of the National Association of Sports Commissions (NASC) has grown by massive proportions. The trend of Destination Marketing Organizations (DMOs) entering the sports tourism and events market has led to a 1,500% growth of the NASC membership since 1992. The strength of this growing tourism sector and its relative immunity to market trends (such as war, a down economy, 9/11, or high unemployment) have driven many DMO leaders to explore the opportunities grass roots events offer to host communities.

In today's economic climate, organizations have to not only do more with less, but often find creative ways to explore new business opportunities (usually without additional resources to support new initiatives). So how can a DMO expand its sports tourism efforts if it's financial and human resources are constant? One west coast CVB created new opportunity for themselves by looking at this issue in a very unique way.

Eugene, Cascades & Coasts Sports (ECCS) is a division of Travel Lane County, the DMO for the greater Eugene, Oregon area. ECCS was created as a new branding effort for the region. Notice I didn't say it was a wholly new sports tourism effort, but a BRANDING initiative. While Eugene didn't build a new sports commission type organization, what they did was unify their existing efforts and resources under a new brand. This gave their region the perception of a centralized sports identity.

Travel Lane County has had some success in the sports tourism space, however they needed the national governing bodies and rights holders to really take notice. They also needed their local community to engage with their efforts in a meaningful way. With their existing resources already allocated (some in sports sales) Travel Lane County decided not to create a wholly new organization, but to brand their existing sports sales efforts in a new way. They created a web site and a logo specific to sports and built an advisory board of local sports leaders. They held a press conference in one of their top sports venues to announce the creation of the ECCS. There was no new line item in their budget for this effort, and no new staff were brought on board. By looking at building a platform around a brand, and not around a completely new budget allocation, Travel Lane County achieved three critical goals through this "new" ECCS:

1. Garnered local interest from media outlets and community leaders.
2. Generated national interest from rights holders and NGBs that led to events being secured for Lane County.
3. The creation of this new brand also led some of their existing members to join the ECCS (in addition to the existing DMO) which led to increased revenues.

So you say "so what, they got creative." This was all done with minimal money spent and no capital investment beyond a new look web page and logo. It was simply an out of the box way of looking at an opportunity.

The moral of this story is that as leaders we need to think how to execute effective campaigns and programs for our stakeholders where opportunities present themselves. Resources or no resources. As sports tourism continues to flourish, there will be more opportunities for DMOs and sports commissions alike. Sometimes we will be able to allocate resources to a new shiny program, sometimes we will need to be as creative as Travel Lane County.

Discussion Questions

1. What opportunities do you have to repackage an existing program to make it more marketable?
2. Talk about your favorite brand in the world. What do you like about it? What can it teach you about your organization?
3. Of the great brands discussed in question number two, what can you borrow from them?

Supplemental Reading

The "Art of Rebranding" is a great short article by Entrepreneur Magazine's John Williams - http://www.entrepreneur.com/article/159470.

XVII

"Your premium brand had better be delivering something special, or it's not going to get the business."
-- Warren Buffett

"Brand or Bust"

While reading the paper to search for something fun to do on a weekend, my wife found an ad for a local renaissance fair. The quarter page ad had a lot of detail, including the event schedule, and photos of some of the characters. The one thing it didn't have? The LOCATION of where the event was taking place.

Having no prior knowledge of this event and its (apparently) long history in our area, we didn't know if it was anywhere near our home in Central Phoenix. So we moved on and chose another activity for the weekend. The ad was a huge miss for the renaissance fair (which apparently is held near Apache Junction, Arizona just in case you were curious). How many others saw the ad, which we assume was quite pricey, and disregarded the event just as we did? There is no way to know, but I am guessing we were not the only ones who grew frustrated with the ad and took our disposable income elsewhere.

The big question is this: How often do we promote our organizations in a way that doesn't have a call to action, or a brand identity that differentiates ourselves from our competitors? I'm sure none of us have ever left out a critical piece of information like an event time or location, or a link to buy tickets, or how to find our web site. However every day, trade publications land in our mailbox with countless print ads that look just like all the others. One has a photo of a kid playing soccer and a pretty picture of a golf course. The next page has a photo touting how great that city is (along with a pretty picture of a golf course and a kid playing soccer). The next page you will find the same ad (insert city name here).

It's our job as sports industry professionals to create differentiation for our products so we can sell more of them. So why run an ad that looks just like everyone else? What assets do you have that nobody else does? Here are some examples of great differentiators.....

- An iconic landmark (like Rapid City and Mount Rushmore)
- History within a sport (think Little League Baseball and Williamsport)
- Legendary coaches or athletes (we bet you know where Muhammad Ali is from)
- Event anniversaries (2015 was the 35 year anniversary of the Miracle on Ice in Lake Placid – they hosted all the living players for a very high profile ceremony)
- Historic venues (there is only one Wrigley, one Lambeau, one Fenway)

By creatively leveraging the unique attributes of your event or your community, you create brand leverage against the competition. How are you utilizing your unique attributes? What makes you different than the town next door? Are you running print ads with non-descript soccer kids and vanilla golf courses, or are you hosting chalk talks with Coach K at Cameron Indoor Stadium? Okay, maybe Coach K is out of reach, but the point remains. Are you playing the same game like everyone else or are you using the assets you have to build a brand?

Discussion Questions

1. What differentiators does your organization/product/destination possess?
2. How can you creatively market those differentiators?
3. What is stopping you from doing it?

Supplemental Reading

Marketing expert Jack Trout wrote one the seminal books on differentiation in marketing titled "Differentiate or Die" – http://www.amazon.com/Differentiate-Die-Survival-Killer-Competition/dp/0470223391/ref=dp_ob_title_bk.

XVIII

"Marketing is no longer about the stuff that you make, but about the stories you tell."
-- Seth Godin

"Marketing Creatively: Reaching New Audiences"

One of the best sports marketing books ever written is "Marketing Outrageously" by Jon Spoelstra. While more recently connected to the sports industry as the father of an NBA coach (his son is NBA Champion Miami Heat coach Erik Spoelstra), Jon was a trailblazer in sports marketing throughout his career. He fathered the strategy of marketing the visiting team's stars to sell tickets, developed the ticket sales call center model, and on more than one occasion mailed renewal notices to season ticket holders via Fed-Ex tied to a rubber chicken (a story worthy of buying the book to read). The case studies and lessons that are outlined in the book provide great insights into the creative thought process in how to develop a unique and compelling message to reach new audiences.....Be that a team, a brand, or in the case of one of our partners, a national governing body of sport.

In 2013, USA BMX engaged our team at the Huddle Up Group to lead four major projects. One of the project areas was to strengthen the USA BMX Foundation and to develop programs that could deliver the sport of BMX to new audiences. Our objective was to reach kids that had likely never been involved in the sport and to do so in a fiscally responsible manner. Our team kicked around numerous ideas such as running free BMX camps, reaching out to youth groups, and marketing through major youth targeted media outlets. The key question that we kept coming back to was this: How does the program SUSTAIN itself? Not only financially, but how can we build a concept that will, on its own volition, create enthusiastic foot soldiers that can carry our brand farther than we could on our own. Enter the USA BMX STEM Program.

Science Technology Engineering and Math (STEM) is one of the hot topics in education right now and rightfully so. Internationally, among the industrialized nations of the world, the United States ranks 25th in math and 17th in science. In recent years, STEM programs have been a major focus of the White House and the Department of Education, including the creation of "Change the Equation," developed by the Obama administration. This new non-profit has a full-time staff dedicated to mobilizing the business community and improving the quality of STEM education in the United States. In a day where PlayStation and Xbox are default choices for kids with free time, well designed STEM programs have started to take root. Instead of having kids sit and play video games, we owe it to our young people to create interesting programs that give them the tools to learn for the future. (Author's note: did you know the "PlayStation" is actually IN spellcheck as a word? This is what we are up against.)

One of our partners at the Huddle Up Group, Mike Duvarney, has been a national leader in the youth programming industry for many years. He knew that STEM was generating a lot of buzz and thought that if we were to launch a new and unique youth outreach effort, STEM might be the right outlet for USA BMX. We designed a program that would have four primary goals:

1. Serve as equal part education, equal part athletics and exercise.

2. Reach a new audience that our USA BMX member tracks likely would not have reached in the past.
3. Promote safe and fun activity for kids that met Common Core standards.
4. Become financially self-sustaining at the end of year one.

As with any great endeavor, we needed the support of people with influence that shared our vision. We built partnerships with some smart university scientists to help develop the curriculum, secured a bike manufacturer to help with the necessary equipment, and contracted with a national sales outlet named STEMFinity.com. We also spent a significant amount of time internally building support with our team members within USA BMX. As part of the program that was developed, each student receives 16-plus hours of STEM education (in a classroom or through an afterschool/extended day program), learns how a bike works and the science behind it, and in the end they earn a free one-day membership to USA BMX. The program formally launched at the National After School Association Conference in February 2013 with a goal of selling ten STEM packages (50 bikes) that would reach 1,500 kids in year number one.

Reaching back to the lessons of Jon Spoelstra, we marketed the program through new channels. Instead of taking the sports program to the sports community (such as PE teachers and parks and rec program leaders), we took our STEM program to the education community (school administrators and teachers). We marketed BMX in a different way to a different audience. As we would soon find out this new audience was keen to the idea of using BMX bikes to attract and retain kids in their after school programs.

Over the first eight months of the program we delivered 250 bikes and reached over 5,000 youth from Sarasota to Spokane. By the end of year two, we had sold over 1,500 bikes to 150 schools nationwide, and the program reached more than 10,000 youth. If we were a retail outlet, the program would rank as one of the top independent bike sellers in the United States. The original program was targeted at youth aged seven to 14, due to the early success we will soon develop both a high school and an under-7 model. This effort has also spawned a sister program for parks and recreation departments in 2016.

The USA BMX STEM Program is financially self-sufficient and has reached more new riders than we could have ever imagined in its first year. While this program has prospects to grow even more in the future, we need to remember how we got here. We attacked the task with a Jon Spoelstra-type mentality: We built a plan geared towards a NON-sports community, we built a solid team of supporters, and we executed the roll-out strategy on time and on budget with an eye on ROI -- more kids on bikes, less on PlayStation (even if it is on spell check). Most importantly, we thought about our brand in a whole new light, with an education lens rather than a sports one.

How does your destination message what you contribute to the community? Do you issue press releases on economic impact and room nights? Do the influencers in your community understand the value proposition you are selling? If not, take a step back. Talk to some smart people from outside your industry and tell them your story. They will ask unique questions and likely offer you insights into ways to sell your brand and your successes in a unique and Jon Spoelstra-type way. They may even suggest the use of rubber chickens.

Discussion Questions

1. Brainstorm five ways you could market your company/destination/organization outrageously.
2. If nobody could say "no" to your new marketing ideas, which one would you launch today?
3. What's stopping you?

XIX

"Those who say, 'That's the way we have always done it' can be the most dangerous people in any company."
-- Kevin Plank

Sticky Sports Tourism

Sports tourism professionals often times battle for "credit." Convention bureaus, sports commissions, and other DMOs often fight each other to validate their work and to scrap for limited community resources. Room night goals, economic impact projections, ROI. Everything that can be measured is often used to validate an organization publicly.

Community leaders often stand in our offices asking for quantifying tangible results of our work. Our elected officials and (yes) our bosses, don't want to hear "room nights are often hard to track" or "the event owners didn't deliver." It's on us to make our work understandable for them, and to translate our results into their language.

The biggest issue is that often times our community leaders have a hard time "touching" the economic impact that results from hosting events. To garner the support we need to further our missions, stakeholders need to not only understand the positive occurrences around our events, but to then FUND future efforts to attract more events that positively impact our markets.

There is a great book by the Heath Brothers called "Made to Stick" that can help us in this area to make that connection. The Heath Brothers are a couple of Stanford-Duke-Harvard professors that have studied human behavior and how to communicate to specific audiences in a meaningful way. The main premise in "Made to Stick" is to deliver a message to your target audience that is VISUAL in a language (or picture) they can understand.

Two examples of how the concept of "sticky" messaging has helped me are below.....

In the early years of my career in sports tourism, Tulsa was trying to build a new arena, which required a new tax to be passed by the voters. We failed on two occasions, but once I was gone the BOK Center sprouted out of the ground (but I digress).....When hosting town hall meetings around Tulsa about the initial project, it was apparent to me that in 1999 there was a significant group of anti-tax citizens that wouldn't support our efforts. The community didn't have the stomach to pay for a new development and entertainment district downtown. It was my impression that they were only against our project because they couldn't understand nor "touch" the economic impact it would bring over time. Years later, I understood that our shortfall was in making the message "sticky." The Heath Brothers' book had not been published back then, but we tried anyway.

At that time in Oklahoma, the whole state had a serious road construction problem. Specifically, pot holes. There came a time in Tulsa that the city couldn't repair the pot holes fast enough, and instead would put small orange construction cones IN the potholes rather than fix them. You could play human Frogger and avoid driving your car into the holes, but the holes couldn't get filled. You'd think it would be more efficient to just fix the pot holes, but it wasn't, so orange cones it was. While Frogger is a really fun video game, doing it with your car was less than enjoyable for most Tulsans.

As we continually hit the wall with citizens and elected officials about the arena project and the economic impact that would be generated by hosting events in the new downtown, I realized we had to make it tangible to our audience (aka - "sticky"). I called the city manager in charge of the pot hole issue and asked him what it cost to fix a single pot hole. He said all-in, about $60. From there forward I used the $60 number to talk about how each event we were going after would result in X number of fixed pot holes (Y million dollars of direct visitor spending from an event divided by $60 = X potholes fixed via the event).

In testing this message with a local Rotary Club it resonated IMMEDIATELY. The orange cones they understood, the sales tax revenue from hosting an NCAA championship, they couldn't comprehend. Pot holes was their language, so we had to translate our message into their vernacular.

While we didn't win the vote on the project, we made significant headway, and I learned the lesson of "sticky" messaging. This lesson helps me today in delivering the right information to the influencers around me in a meaningful way.

Another example of this tactic was when we revamped the Phoenix Sports Commission in 2008. We realized early on that the organization needed a major facelift in the community. Leaders in Arizona didn't know what our organization was about and what our value proposition was. They did however understand ROI and how an investment in sports tourism could be measured in economic impact. In early 2009 we launched a campaign called the "$100,000,000 Mission." The object of the 24-month project was to land grass roots sporting events that would generate a NEW $100 million in direct visitor spending. The mission only included events that if the Sports Commission wasn't involved would have never come to the greater Phoenix area. So our value proposition was defined, it was transparent, and community leaders could understand the target. It was "sticky" to them.

As the mission moved along, we updated the community early and often. As we landed each event, we didn't just issue a press release, we issued a messaging statement that talked about where we stood (our running total) on the "Mission." We held ourselves accountable to the community, and as we moved the ball down the field on the project, people got on board. Influential people. People with resources and connections. People who could take the Sports Commission to the next level.

Over time, the organization got noticed and became an asset to the Phoenix community. And when we crossed the finish line on the "Mission" we thanked the community for the investment that had been made for the organization to get there. We also began messaging the financial return of the "Mission" project. Community leaders understand ROI.

Had we not employed a "sticky" concept, I'm not sure we would have achieved what we did. The NASC named the Phoenix Regional Sports Commission the Large Market Sports Commission of the Year in 2012, just four years after our reorganization. The board of the Sports Commission changed dramatically. It became bigger, stronger, and more influential. Through their support, our events had more muscle and the organization more stature in the community. It all started with one transparent and tangible goal that people could understand and get their arms around, and the organization evolved from there.

What are your community leaders saying to you? What don't they understand about your efforts in the sports tourism and events space? What is keeping them from supporting you publicly and privately? Do they understand your value proposition? How can you change the dialog into their language to make your message stick?

Discussion Questions

1. What don't your stakeholders understand about your business?
2. What "languages" do your stakeholders speak?
3. How can you convert your value proposition into a language/message they can understand?

XX

"Always remember that you are absolutely unique. Just like everyone else."
-- Margaret Mead

What's Your Zip Line?
Contributed by Gary Alexander, Principal, Huddle Up Group

In 2012, Indianapolis hosted a very successful Super Bowl. Prior to the game, during Super Bowl week, organizers set up a zip line, right down the middle of their city. This zip line was a steel cable that stretched between two towers. Participants could attach themselves to this cable and slide between the towers for a whole city block, suspended over the street and spectators. The media got engaged and had fun with it. Several celebrities went down the zip line and several, once they got to the top of the zip line starting tower, decided it was a little outside their comfort zone. Coverage of the zip line activities was on television for the entire week. Who would and who wouldn't participate became the talk of the town; it became the talk of the nation.

During that the same time, Nashville was in the middle of preparations for the 2014 National Collegiate Athletic Association (NCAA) Women's Final Four Basketball Tournament, the year-ending culmination of the women's collegiate basketball season. Each year a city, led by a Local Organizing Committee (LOC), hosts six days of parties, events, conferences, and three basketball games. The result at week's end is the crowning of the NCAA Women's Basketball National Champion.

I was honored to serve as the Executive Director of the Local Organizing Committee. It was my responsibility to make sure the event was operationally and financially successful, and just as important, my responsibility to make it memorable for the participants and the fans.

Shortly after the Super Bowl, during one of our LOC staff meetings, I asked our team, "What's our zip line?" What will everyone be talking about, outside of the games? What will be Nashville's signature?"

If you know anything about Nashville, you know we're called Music City. We're home of the Country Music Hall of Fame. Our downtown is lined with live music venues called Honky Tonks. Every June we host the Country Music Association Music Festival. Even our Convention & Visitors Corporation is called, Visit Music City. So as you can imagine, with not much debate, it was decided that in Music City, for the 2014 NCAA Women's Final Four, our zip line had to be music! Therefore, we took it upon ourselves to infuse live music into every activity that we did. We had music at all the special events around the Final Four; at the Governor's Reception, the Championship Luncheon, and at the interactive fan festival called Tourney Town. We had it at the Bounce on Broadway, where 2,500 children and their parents bounced a basketball down the streets of Nashville. Live music was at pre-Game hospitality on both competition days. We even had live performers outside the entrances to the arena for spectators to enjoy on game-days. Everywhere you went, you couldn't help but run into live music. Everyone was talking about how great and how prolific the music was in Nashville! Mission accomplished!

As you read this, you may be thinking, that's fine for Nashville, but we're not Music City. What does that have to do with my community? No, you may not be Music City, but I assure you that your community is unique in its own way. It has assets or traditions on which you can capitalize. When I think of Albuquerque, I think of the Southwestern culture and the balloon festival. St. Louis brings to mind baseball, sportsmanship and the Arch. Denver, the Mile High City, has its mountains and outdoor activities and the Denver Broncos. You may know Wimbledon has a tradition of "strawberries and cream," but did you know that Kalamazoo, Michigan, has had a tradition of "blueberries and cream?" Since 1943, the USTA Boys National Tennis Championships, one of the longest running youth tennis tournaments in the country, has been held in Kalamazoo, and with it a tradition of serving "blueberries and cream." Everywhere, every community, has something that makes it special.

Discover your uniqueness. Brainstorm with your team, brainstorm with your stakeholders, talk to the arts community, the music community, the foodies. You'll be surprised what you'll find. Everyone will have a different perspective of their hometown or the upcoming event. When you find a theme or idea that keeps reoccurring, you will have discovered your zip line!

We often ask our clients, "What unique attributes of your event or your community do you have to create brand leverage against the competition? How are you leveraging your uniqueness? Are you playing the same game like everyone else or are you using the assets you have to build a brand?"

Your zip line can change from event to event, from year to year. The key is to have one, so that as your guests depart, they'll be talking about your community and talking about when they will return to experience and enjoy it again. I challenge you, find your zip line!

Discussion Questions

1. What's going to make your destination/event different from your competitors?
2. Who can you engage and add to your team for an outside perspective?
3. Once you have your zip line, how can you leverage it to sell your destination?

Supplemental Reading

USA Today's Robert Klemko writes about Indianapolis' Zip Line – http://content.usatoday.com/communities/thehuddle/post/2012/01/indy-borrows-zip-line-attraction-from-winter-olympics/1#.VdJfQZd3FT8.

XXI

"Teach thy tongue to say 'I do not know', and thou shalt progress."
-- Maimonides

"Ten Commandments of Sports Tourism"

Americans are big fans of lists. From Letterman's "Top Ten" to the numerous rankings of college sports teams, we love lists. In that spirit, along with some help from sports industry leaders, here are our "Ten Commandments of Sports Tourism" for your destination…...

Thou shalt build sustainable relationships…..From rights holders and governing bodies, to community leaders and local corporate partners, time and resources need to be allocated to continually connect with the people that make our business go. Make time each day for outreach efforts. As John David, Chief Operating Officer of USA BMX points out, "In a partnership everyone wins. Strive to always develop partnerships and the business will repeat!"

Thou shalt not bid on one-off events…..Recreating the wheel over and over makes it difficult to build a sustainable sports tourism business. Seek out partners that will work with you over multiple years so you can build on success from year to year and ensure a stable amount of tourism for your community.

Thou shalt do due diligence before responding to an RFP…..Before spending time and energy on a bid, reach out to your peers. Call members of the National Association of Sports Commissions and gain feedback. John David advises, "The devil is always in the details, find out the details before you commit." A little research now could save you a lot of pain later.

Thou shalt bid to win.....There are sales managers that will bid on an event with no intent to win. It's likely that they are just trying to drive their sales or lead response numbers. This happens more than you think, and event owners know who these cities are. Event owners talk just like host cities do, and this practice gets a lot of air time. If you don't want to host the event, spend your time and energy elsewhere.

Thou shalt control the dialog.....A major pet peeve of many event owners is to get inundated with calls from hoteliers. It makes the DMO look like they have limited control of their local folks, which over time will wear thin with the rights holders. Communicate early and often to your local hoteliers that if they have questions about an event to contact you directly. The DMO should take the lead in talking to the event owners at all times.

Thou shalt not pay bid fees for an unproven event.....I've been burned by this one in the past. There is plenty of business out there through events with proven track records. Focus on the proven, let others chase the untested.

Thou shalt not bid on an event through a broker.....This is happening more and more in our industry. Third parties are representing rights holders in bid processes, often times without the knowledge of the rights holder. If you are solicited by a third party, ask the rights holder if you are to work with the third party or deal with them directly. Clear and direct communication with the event owner is always the best route.

Here are two from Matt Ten Haken, Sports Sales Manager for the Fox Cities Convention & Visitors Bureau (thanks Matt!!!!).....

Honor thy volunteers.....It would be impossible to pull off most of your major events without volunteers, so treat them well. Respect their time, give them enough to eat and drink, keep them as comfortable as possible, and give them important tasks. But you need to draw the line. Some volunteers will demand too much of you or try to take on more

66

than they are suited for. Keep them in check, but still respect how important they are for the event.

Thou shalt not compete against your neighbor's events.....Some of the best events that Fox Cities has hosted came from a partnership with a neighboring community. You can host a good event with your own resources, but often times you can host a GREAT event when joining forces with others. If you work together rather than compete against your neighbors, partnering on the larger events can prove beneficial for all involved.

The final commandment, one that I feel is critically important.....

Thou shalt be transparent to your constituents.....It's imperative to be open and honest with your partners at all times. In order to sustain your organization's efforts, you will need to garner support from rights holders, local leaders, sponsors, elected officials, volunteers, and related entities. Successful leaders realize that long-term success relies on an open dialog built on collaboration and trust. Make time to communicate with your various constituent groups in a consistent and meaningful way. Put reminders in your outlook, host quarterly mixers, have coffee with your key volunteers once a year. However you manage your outreach efforts, make it meaningful, and carry it out with consistent precision. Your constituents will remember your efforts and will feel their voices have been heard when key issues arise.

There are many more commandments we could add to this list.

Discussion Questions

1. These commandments were written from the host city side of the industry. If you were to craft your top five commandments from the event rights holder side of the sports events business, what would you include?
2. What commandments would you add to the above list?

3. If you have a list of guiding principles in your organization, how are they communicated?

Supplemental Reading

Author Barry Moltz outlines his commandments for growing a small business -https://www.americanexpress.com/us/small-business/openforum/articles/the-10-commandments-of-growing-a-business/.

XXII

"Most organizations spend their time marketing to the crowd. Smart organizations assemble the tribe."
-- Seth Godin

"Bridge Building in Sports"

The future of the sports tourism and events industry is in your hands. As a professional in this space, you have the ability to participate in one of the fastest growing tourism markets of all time. In a day of increasing competition, how will you differentiate yourself (and your organization) from all the others? No matter how you answer that question, your ability to build positive relationships, and thusly influence, will heavily impact your future success.

In the future, new players will enter the fray, accountability standards (ROI) will rise, and the professionalism of our industry will continue become more structured. As these phenomena continue, the personal relationships we develop will make or break many careers. With that in mind, here are four ways to create lasting relationships in the sports industry.

1. Develop a value proposition – What is it that you can offer a partner that others cannot? As a host city, do you have better venues, a strong volunteer base, or the ability to raise sponsorship dollars? As a rights holder, can you offer vast media exposure, drive hotel room occupancy, or help leave a legacy behind when your event is over? Each side of the equation needs to define and present to the other the value add they bring to the table.

2. Be visible – People do business with those they trust. One can develop a reputation as an authority by frequently participating in industry events, sitting on panels, writing topical blogs, etc. The key is to be consistent in this effort.

3. Engage your network – Whatever way you decide to communicate with your network, make sure your message with them is clear. The more they know about your value proposition (from #1 above) and your goals, the more empowered they will be to help you along the way. Once again, consistency in communication is key.

4. Be prepared – Once you have achieved a trust amongst your peers in the industry, and are routinely engaging your network, there will come a time when these contacts will reach out to you for your help. When that happens, you must be ready when called upon. Some of the biggest events/projects we have ever worked on happened when a partner called to say they needed help. As you build professional bridges, when they can bear fruit, you have to be ready and responsive.

There is an old saying, "The only bad thing about burning bridges behind you is that the world is round." Of course the implication is that as relationships evolve, some will not end well. At the same time, if you invest your personal resources in building your network professionally, positive things will come from this effort.

As with any great endeavor, to be successful requires vigilant planning and proper execution. Build a game plan around your value add, put the plan out in the open, communicate with your network, and be ready when called upon. Whether they know it or not, the best leaders in our industry employ these four tenets to achieve success, and so can you.

Our industry is in your hands, so use these four steps to build bridges for the future.

Discussion Questions

1. What is your organization's value proposition?
2. What is your personal value proposition?
3. How are you visible in your community? Nationally? Internationally?

Supplemental Reading

"Tribes" by Seth Godin is one the top books in the business field. There is also a related TED talk –
http://www.ted.com/talks/seth_godin_on_the_tribes_we_lead?language=en.

XXIII

"If you don't try to win you might as well hold the Olympics in somebody's back yard."
-- Jesse Owens

"Bids Without Boarders"

As I was watching the 2014 Winter Olympics in Sochi, media outlets all over the world were predicting where future Games will be held. The next three host cities include summer hosts Rio (2016) and Tokyo (2020), and 2018 winter site Pyeongchang, South Korea. Beyond that, it's anyone's guess. The United States did not submit a 2022 Winter Olympics bid, however there seems to be interest in the 2024 Summer Games process -- including a unique dual-host bid by San Diego and Tijuana.

This is not the first time a joint bid has been presented. While at the time of this writing the International Olympic Committee (IOC) doesn't provide for dual city bids (let alone one from multiple countries), the concept is one worth a second look. If the Olympic Games aren't the platform to show international unity between two host countries, then I'm not sure one exists. (Author's note: In December of 2014 the IOC took strides to open the door for multi-country bids in the future).

The governing document for the Games, the Olympic Charter, identifies the objectives of the IOC are to "to promote Olympism throughout the world and to lead the Olympic Movement." The Charter also talks about promoting ethics as well as encouraging and supporting the development of sport. The document goes further in article six to state, "The Olympic

Games are competitions between athletes in individual or team events and not between countries." Excellent. Now that it's not about one country against another, why can't two countries come together to host the games as one?

San Diego and Tijuana are not alone, there are other destinations that could work across borders to host a mega-event. Detroit and Windsor (Canada) already work together on some events. The Indonesia–Malaysia–Singapore Growth Triangle was created for regional partnership. As a territory, Hong Kong would need the support of China's mainland. Switzerland, France and Germany have numerous transborder conurbations (a fancy term for places with several large cities in one area that lie in different countries).

There are opportunities, but as we know the Olympic movement is often slow to, well, move. Rather than wait for the IOC, if we want to show the world that sport is indeed the platform to show unity, we must take action. Until two communities come together to host a mega event on the word's stage, we won't ever have an example to point to and stir the discussion. Someone must take the first step, find a dance partner, and host something that is flawless in its execution and spectacular in its partnership. Who wants to go first?

Discussion Questions

1. Describe a time when your organization crossed borders (not merely geographic ones) to partner on a project.
2. What positives and negatives came from the partnership?
3. In what ways can you work with your neighbors that would transcend your community?

XXIV

"When there is a rush for everyone to do the same thing, it becomes more difficult to do."
-- Mark Cuban

"Break the Mold"

As we consult destinations on their sports tourism efforts, we are often asked to evaluate a community's venue offering. In this process, we work to identify differentiating opportunities for the creation of new venues or the enhancement of existing facilities. While every host community is different in some way, we often find the same issues bubbling up from one destination to the next.

Here are the top three.....

1. Silos – As in the corporate world, we often find that even the smallest communities have significant communication issues. This leads to various city divisions or community groups operating independently from one another. Consistent and open communication between stakeholders is key in achieving success for a host city.
2. Redundancy – Expanding on the first item, if you work in silos it would make sense that one town doesn't know what the other is doing and thusly may build the exact same things. In areas where there are multiple jurisdictions, it is common to find redundant sports facilities from one city to the next. This most often happens when a community thinks only about their local users and not the region as a whole. The best regional efforts have solid communication on what facilities are needed, and they participate together in the long-range master planning process.
3. "Community" First – Most cities think about their citizens ("community users") first, and give little thought to the impact their venues could make in attracting large national tournaments.

In the case of parks and recreation departments, this is understandable. After all, most parks systems are funded by the local taxpayer and cities build venues and program them for that taxpayer. On the flip side, you can make a case that very few parks programs generate enough revenue to pay for themselves (most are subsidized), while hosting a major national tournament draws in significant tourism spending which in the end helps the community as a whole. The "community user versus tourism focus" is a debate we see in nearly every city with whom we work. In the end, there must be a balance between the two in order to maximize the positive impacts on a city or geographic region.

Orson Welles once said that to be successful, one should "Create your own visual style... let it be unique for yourself and yet identifiable for others." We interpret this to say: don't be like the Joneses next door. Develop a differentiated offering, and present your "uniqueness" to the marketplace.

In the sports tourism and events industry, it's easy to pull together a non-descript collateral piece, attend a few trade shows, field a bunch of RFPs, hang out with the same people from one show to the next, and to just be like everyone else. As leaders, we must aspire for more. We must find ways to break the mold and dare to be different. Use an RFP as a discussion starter rather than a finite document. Go out of your way at trade shows to meet with new sports organizations, not just those you already work with. Split up at the keynote luncheon and sit with people from different geographic regions. Find a way to make your FAM unlike anyone else's. Push the envelope, dare to be unique, and break the mold for success.

Discussion Questions

1. What is unique about your organization/destination?
2. How do you promote that uniqueness?
3. Who is the most unique person/destination/company in your space? What makes them special?

XXV

"I not only use all the brains that I have, but all that I can borrow."
-- Woodrow Wilson

"Lemons into Lemonade, Sports Event Awesome"

One of my favorite public speakers is a Canadian author-blogger-tweeter named Scott Stratten. Scott has an unwavering dedication to tell stories of business "Awesome." He spreads the gospel where people across the world take work situations that look like lemons and turn them into lemonade. Below is a personal story from my experiences in running sporting events. We can call this a case study for "Sports Events Awesome" (trademark pending, unless Scott already has it).

In 2001, I was fortunate to be the event director of the Western Athletic Conference Basketball tournament in Tulsa, Oklahoma. The WAC as it is known, was a great league back then. Some of the legends of college basketball coached in the league (including Jerry Tarkanian, Billy Tubbs, and Don Haskins) and the level of play was elite even on the worst nights. However one small conversation that week in Tulsa forever shaped how I look at opportunities to enrich an event, and it had nothing to do with the basketball court.

During the event we had our travel agency housed within the arena. They had their own in house television feed of the games going on in the building, and as teams appeared to be poised to get knocked out of the tournament, the travel agents started booking outbound flights for them. At the time Tulsa's airport didn't offer many opportunities to get 20-30 people out of town on a moment's notice, so the travel agents were busy trying to find options quickly as teams were eliminated (the Tulsa airport is MUCH better and bigger now, FYI). As you can guess, when teams get knocked out of a tournament, coaches often don't want to hang around town when they have lost, they can be cranky like that. So our goal was to get them home as quickly as we could when they were eliminated.

The travel agency was also responsible for getting bands and cheerleaders out of town when their basketball teams lost as well. This is where the AWESOME occurred.......The University of Texas at El Paso (UTEP) lost a close game in the semi-finals late Friday night. The travel agency got the basketball team on a plane early Saturday morning to head home, but there were no seats available to get the band back to Texas. The band had flights booked for Sunday, and they were going to have to stay in Tulsa for two more days. A call came over the radio for me to report to the travel office. I assumed that a coach was waiting for me to express their displeasure about not getting an immediate flight out of town, but when I arrived in the office, it was a completely different conversation that awaited me.

The band director for UTEP was there, and I was brought up to speed on their plight (having to stay in Tulsa two more nights). The band director however had asked for me to come talk to him not because he was upset, but because he wanted to be Awesome.......One of the member schools in the WAC back then was the University of Hawaii. Hawaii had defeated UTEP on that Friday night. Due to the high costs of housing and travel, Hawaii rarely had their band travel with them to the mainland for road games. UTEP's band director noticed this and posed a question to me, "Hawaii didn't bring their band did they?" I confirmed that they hadn't. He then said, "Well, we are here until Sunday, can we play for them in the championship game tomorrow night?" I wasn't sure I understood what he was saying, as I had NEVER heard of a rival school's band supporting another team. So after he clarified that they would like to literally play FOR Hawaii, I looked around the room and said, "why not?"

On my way to the arena that Saturday night, I did have concerns about what they would be wearing, and how they would actually represent Hawaii. As soon as I walked in, those concerns calmed immediately.

The UTEP band took their place in the north end of the arena (Hawaii's designated section), with a national television audience tuning in on ESPN. In seats that would likely have been empty, they filled in the section for Hawaii's band and really added to the atmosphere of the event.

The band director (being Awesome on his own volition), had gone to Wal-Mart that day, and bought 20 reasonably priced Hawaiian button down shirts in pastel colors. He also scored some flower necklaces that played the part of the Hawaiian lei. So come game time (and ESPN time) they looked the part. And the topper of it all, was when the Hawaii team came running out of the tunnel to take the court, the band keyed up and played the TV theme song to Hawaii Five-O (Dah-dahnana-nah-na, dah-dahnana- na....).

As I went over to thank the UTEP band's director (in near tears I might add), I said, "I have to ask, how did you think of the Five-O song?" He said they were happy to participate in the championship game and commented about their musical selection, "We don't know their fight song, so it's the closest thing we had."

I said "AWESOME."

This is a great example of how to take a negative event and turn it into a win-win outcome for all involved. The band had a good time, the arena had an improved atmosphere, and I'm sure the Hawaii team appreciated the added support. The practice of bands playing for competing schools has since become a tradition in the WAC. It all started with one band leader looking at a situation in a very different way.

We all have opportunities for "Sports Event Awesome", let's make sure when the moment arrives, we are ready to take advantage of them!

Discussion Questions

1. Talk about instance when you have experienced "Sports Events Awesome."
2. How can you perpetuate Sports Events Awesome in your organization?
3. Who is the most Awesome organization in your industry? What stops you from being like them?

XXVI

"The most important thing in communication is to hear what isn't being said."
-- Peter Drucker

"Bid Presentations: Hitting a Home Run"

Many of the articles we have published talk about the importance of an open dialog with your partners. In many instances, the answers they give you can lead you to success. Specific to the sports tourism industry, the insights you gain be used to craft a winning strategy in bidding to host major events in your communities. Here is one example of how intel obtained from a rights holder helped us land a high profile championship in Denver.....

In 2005 while at the Metro Denver Sports Commission, we were simultaneously building a bid to host the 2008 Frozen Four and a future Women's Final Four. As is often the case, we attended the events as observers each year leading up to our bids. Obviously anything we could pick up as an onlooker that would differentiate our city would be helpful. Denver is a hotbed for hockey at all levels, so we focused in on landing the Frozen Four.

Throughout the process we asked the rights holder (the NCAA), past host cities, coaches, players, media, fans and anyone else who would listen, "What would make this event a Home Run in Denver?" In the case of the Frozen Four it became obvious there were two issues that needed to be addressed.

First, the ice in the host facility had been inconsistent year to year. This was mainly due to the presence of an NHL team in the hosting arenas. The logistics of melting the ice down after an NHL game, repainting the NCAA marks and logos on the ice, and then refreezing the surface was a tedious one. In order for the ice to be of perfect texture, you had to have people skating on it for days to break it in by the time the Frozen Four teams arrived. This process was often compressed due to the NHL team playing a game in the latest possible window prior to the Frozen Four and thus making it hard to get the ice conditioned properly.

The second issue was also related to an NHL tenant. In one of the past host cities of the Frozen Four, there was an NHL team that used the building and they were (to put it nicely) less than hospitable in giving up their arena for the week of the tournament. Numerous people within the collegiate hockey community explained to us how this team had actually gone out of their way to make the Frozen Four staff feel less than welcome. This included not allowing the tournament to use their locker room for one of the collegiate teams. The NHL team also blocked access to their area of the arena (including NCAA staff, media, the Frozen Four's teams and ESPN - the tournament's broadcast partner). This was not an ideal situation and from a community standpoint, the Frozen Four was a big deal, so there was a major disconnect.

As we put together our bid, we realized the two big issues for the NCAA Committee (that would be deciding the future host sites for the tournament) were really both tied to the NHL team in the venue. We decided to sit down with the leadership of the Colorado Avalanche who called Denver's Pepsi Center home. We would need their help in alleviating the concerns of an NHL tenant in a Frozen Four building if we were to win the bid for 2008.

The President of the Avalanche at that time was Pierre Lacqroix. Pierre is a legend in hockey and is very well respected in the sports industry. We explained the issues the NCAA had in another city and asked for his formal support of our bid. At the time the Avs were winning (a lot), and consistently competing for the Stanley Cup (they had won the Cup in 1996 and 2001). Pierre not only took a position of support for our effort, but he went one step further.....He offered to move the Avalanche out of the building entirely should we host the 2008 Frozen Four.

At that time the first round of the NHL playoffs were held the same week as the Frozen Four. The NHL playoffs were best of five in round one, so the net effect of Pierre's offer was that if the Avalanche were the better seed in the playoffs, they would go on the road in games one and two as the visiting team. In a day when sports was becoming big business, this was a MAJOR commitment on behalf of the Avalanche.

While the ice issue was a big one (we solved that by scheduling youth teams to hold a 24 hour skate on the new ice), the NHL presence was the linchpin. We went into the NCAA bid with a letter from Pierre outlining their commitment to embrace the Frozen Four in Denver and to step aside should we be awarded the event. The NCAA Hockey Committee members were floored. Nobody had ever gone to that extent to garner a commitment of that magnitude. We were awarded the event, as well as an NCAA Regional in 2007. The committee thanked us for the level of support we were offering to their championship, and we went to work on creating a truly memorable event.

The 2007 NCAA Western Hockey Regional and the 2008 Frozen Four both set ticket and revenue records for the time. The events were both viewed in our community as smashing successes and established Denver as a home for major hockey events. Had we not asked the "Home Run" question, I'm not sure we would have had the ammunition to land these prestigious events. While the support of Pierre and the Avs cannot be overlooked, had we not dug deep into the DNA of the event and its history, we would never have known what to ask our community leaders to support.

Ask your partners what they need, ask them for the "Home Run", then go make it happen and put on the best event your community has ever hosted. Then repeat the cycle again and again, and keep hitting home runs.

Discussion Questions

1. Discuss an event bid that you lost because you didn't ask the "Home Run" question.
2. With a partner/colleague, role play the "Home Run" question with one of you playing the host community and one of you playing the event rights holder.
3. Outline a situation where your organization hit a "Home Run" and how you arrived at that outcome.

XXVII

"Life isn't about finding yourself. Life is about creating yourself."
-- George Bernard Shaw

Created Events – Richmond Sports Backers

Over the past few years several sports commissions and even some convention bureaus have entered into the event creation business. While some have struggled, others have had success in this space. By creating their own events destinations are developing assets that they can have more control over, including when the events happen, where they take place, and how the profits and losses are handled. Through event creation the event owner (in this case the destination) can build championships that fit their venues, fill open calendar dates, and provide year over year tourism consistency. Often times, bidding on existing events provides only some of these key benefits.

In the United States, there are over 400 destinations that are active in the sports tourism marketplace. Each player in this space falls somewhere on the event strategy continuum, from hosting all bid-in (existing) events, to a mix of bid-in and created events, to running all created events. Most host cities fall somewhere in the middle of the continuum with a tendency to be closest to the bid-in hosting strategy. Historically, a heavy event creation strategy was the extreme end of the spectrum, with very few "outlier" cities playing in that area of the industry. The prime example of a community that has generated significant success in the event creation model for driving sports tourism is the City of Richmond, Virginia and the Richmond Sports Backers.

Sports Backers Executive Director Jon Lugbill, a former World Champion whitewater canoe slalom racer, shared with us the history of the Sports Backers and their vision for creating events. In our interview, Mr. Lugbill outlined the genesis of their success. The story goes something like this…..

In 1998 the Richmond Sports Backers was a struggling non-profit organization. They had challenges financially and were attempting to find their long-term direction. At that same time, the local newspaper decided to discontinue the Richmond Marathon which they had run for several years. The Marathon had 2,000 runners at that time, and while modest in participation, was widely recognized by the community as a popular event. As necessity is often the mother of invention, it was at this time that the Sports Backers Board of Directors decided to discontinue the planning and production of fundraising events and focus on created events – including taking over the Richmond Marathon. The Marathon would grow in 13 of the 15 years that followed and today is a cornerstone event for the Sports Backers and the Richmond community (over 19,000 runners participated in the 2013 event).

The Sports Backers added a 10K race in 2000. The inaugural year there were 2,500 runners, and participation in this event doubled each of the following two years. With the Marathon growing and the 10K tracking successfully, the organization decided to double down on their event creation efforts. In 2001 the Board of Directors voted on a strategic plan to create one new event each year for the next five years. This plan would require a significant fundraising effort, and the knowledge that the newly created events would likely lose money in the first two years before becoming profitable. The fundraising campaign raised $1.8 million through private companies and an additional $750,000 from government agencies. The key in the sales process was the vision that over time, events would be created that would drive tourism to Richmond, while enhancing the quality of life for its citizens, year after year.

In the final year of the strategic plan (2006), the Sports Backers added an incubator program to assist local event promoters in growing their sports tourism and event efforts. These strategic partnerships increased the overall economic impact on the area and created a more tactical community approach to hosting sporting events. Through increased communication and collaboration, the community's events generated significantly more benefit than in working independently of one another.

The Sports Backers have continued to create new championships each year and now operate 15 events annually, while also supporting ten (10) additional competitions through the incubator program. With a focus on created events with individual participants (and not team tournaments) the organization found that scaling capacity as registrations increased was much more manageable. In 2013 the Sports Backers created events had over 85,000 participants and an additional 300,000 spectators. Today, the Sports Backers have 26 full-time employees and an annual budget of $7.1 million (86% of their revenues come from registrations at their created events).

While the Richmond Sports Backers still do bid-in a handful of events each year, event creation is their bread and butter. The Sports Backers are the industry leader in the created event trend and their vision in 1998 has served them well as today's marketplace tries to catch up. In our interview with Mr. Lugbill, we asked him what recommendations he would have to those that were considering a shift towards a more created sports event/tourism strategy. Here is a summary of what he said:

- To be good, the organization and its leaders need to be entrepreneurial. A bid-in event strategy requires a different expertise based on sales. A created event strategy requires an entrepreneurial vision.
- The event creation strategy can be very successful in markets that don't have professional sports teams. In a case like Richmond there is less competition for media coverage which makes garnering community support more attainable (note: Richmond has no tier-one sports teams, but there is a NASCAR track).

The Sports Backers and their supporters have built quite a business in Richmond. Sports tourism there is not only an economic driver but hosting and participating in events is a way of life. I'm sure many people who read this case study will look at the numbers (15 events, $7.1 million budget, 26 staff, etc.) and say "that is out of reach for us, those numbers are unattainable." One need only look back at the state of the Sports Backers in 1998. The organization was unstable, unsustainable, and was struggling for a vision – it was a dire state.

If the Richmond Sports Backers can go from where they were 15 years ago to the industry leader they are today, so can you. We recommend that your community look at a created event strategy. Seek out collaborative partnerships that leverage your community assets. Build a sustainable event, then another, then repeat. In Hawaii there is a saying, "Hana Hou" which means "one more time." There is opportunity for Hana Hou in creating events in your communities. All we must do is start.

Discussion Questions

1. What opportunities does your community have to start a new sporting event or festival?
2. What resources would you need to launch the event (human and financial capital)?
3. What events do you currently have in your market that you can help enhance and grow for the future?

Supplemental Reading

Every created event needs a marketing strategy. Here is a link to a Jay Baker article on how to use social media to market your events – http://www.convinceandconvert.com/social-media-marketing/7-ways-to-use-social-media-to-create-buzzworthy-events/.

XXVIII

"Conversation about the weather is the last refuge of the unimaginative."
-- Oscar Wilde

"Compete vs. Collaborate"

Famous psychiatrist Carl Jung once said, "Synchronicity is an ever present reality for those who have eyes to see." In the hyper-competitive world of tourism marketing, three cities had the vision to capture an opportunity.

In 2014, three major convention cities, San Antonio, Baltimore, and Anaheim, partnered together to sell their destinations collectively to the larger national conferences. This collaboration, titled "Synchrocities", offers potential clients some unique benefits in working with these three cities.

Here are three great advantages these cities share in this partnership:

1. Knowledge – By booking with all three cities, the rights holder can ensure a knowledge transfer from one Synchrocity to the next. This will cut down on the learning curve of hosting a new event, and will result in a superior event for the attendees.
2. Pricing – It's quite likely there are areas of cost savings that can be achieved by booking with three cities at one time. The least of which would be the ability to leverage the major hotel brands by bidding out the hotel blocks for all three cities at one time rather than as one-off events. Additional savings can be captured by bundling the purchasing power for all three events in the areas of convention services, event operations, signage production, awards and communications to name just a few.
3. Sponsorship – By bundling an event in three major markets such as those in the Synchrocities, there is great opportunity to sell all

three events as one in the rights holder's sponsorship packages. Especially in this case where the Synchrocities are large markets, sponsors would likely see added value in buying all three destinations at once versus fielding solicitations from each city individually.

There have been examples in the sports tourism and events industry of organizations working together as well. It's common for DMOs partner together on sales trips, several destinations have partnered together to form regional sports marketing groups, and some sports organizations have even banded together to lobby for changes in state laws and for increased funding.

Helen Keller once said, "Alone we can do so little, together we can do so much." The key takeaway is this…. If you have the vision and the guts to step outside of the norm, to bring in partners and collaborate, there are great rewards at the end of the journey.

Discussion Questions

1. Discuss examples where your organization has partnered with others. What were the outcomes of the partnership?
2. What opportunities exist where you could partner with another organization in your market that would be beneficial to you?
3. List the ways in which your organization would benefit from partnering with another entity.

Supplemental Readings

Author/researcher Rick Lash offers a great paper on the art of collaboration, titled "The Collaboration Imperative – http://iveybusinessjournal.com/publication/the-collaboration-imperative/.